CONTENTS

✍ **W9-AFF-844**

PREFACE

In past research, I have noticed a lack of information about the police sniper. There are ample books pertaining to weapons, equipment, training, and philosophies about military sniping, and the various military branches possess a wealth of knowledge in this arena. But many of these concepts require modification for use in the civilian sector. Our present litigious society that thrives on vicarious liability settlements necessitates limitations on Special Weapons and Tactics (SWAT) snipers that the military doesn't consider. One sure way a SWAT team can find itself embroiled in criminal, civil, or social difficulties is to operate along purely military lines.

There are definite differences between military and paramilitary operations. The military emphasizes long-range rifle fire against a wide variety of specified targets and targets of opportunity. A killing shot is as good as a wounding shot, since either will remove an enemy from action. There are no hostages or victims whose welfare is endangered by a miss or a wounding shot. Identification of the target is not as critical as it is in civilian law enforcement. Normally, the military is not concerned with questions of authority to act, criminal and civil liabilities, innocent bystanders, or the necessity to justify its actions in court.

The mission of the law enforcement sniper is more specific and controlled. The law enforcement sniper is trained in marksmanship, fieldcraft, and observation techniques. He delivers precision fire on identified targets upon command. Operations are conducted in permissive civilian environments that are open to all where indiscriminate destruction is not allowed. The law enforcement sniper must be absolutely sure of the identity of any target to be engaged. This is the single factor that governs the range in which the law enforcement sniper can engage a target, and positive identification is difficult, at best, at ranges in excess of 200 yards. The police sniper must operate within the law and accept the fact that his operations may be reviewed in court. Many departments are reluctant to even identify snipers as such. They are called precision riflemen, scout riflemen, sierra teams, or open-air assaulters. These labels are used to soften perceptions in court.

The intent of this book is to aid sniper commanders and sniper team leaders in police sniper operations. Philosophies on sniper preparation, planning, primary and secondary duties, deployment, coordination, and control are covered. Decide what techniques you will train your snipers to use in relation to your specific tactical environment. I sincerely hope this book will serve as a source of guidance and assistance in performing the toughest SWAT task of all: sniping.

ACKNOWLEDGMENTS

Many people made this book possible. Here is a rough list of people I'd like to send heartfelt thank-yous: John Austerman, Mark Andronis, Dave Bowman, Greg Chattin, Charles Douglas, Garry Hager, Bob Jindra, Ron Knauff, Randy McGinnis, Bill Overly, Rich Parker, Bob Schmidt, and Gary Souders—all former sniper team members; Jim Ephlin, a fine armorer who kept the teams' weapons in peak condition; and sundry unnamed fellow instructors in the Federal Bureau of Investigations (FBI), the Department of Energy (DOE), the Department of Defense (DOD), and civilian police sectors.

CHAPTER ONE

HOW SHOULD THE SNIPER BE EQUIPPED?

It's sometimes difficult to understand administrators who are more interested in purchasing high-tech audiovisual equipment than top-quality Federal .308 match rounds. As a sniper commander, I have fought numerous battles for the SWAT officers on the firing line with these bureaucrats and, for the most part, have been successful using the following technique.

First, the sniper commander should act concerned about the budget and express his appreciation for the procurement officer's talents in handling such a tough assignment. (This is also called sucking, but sniper commanders must do what they have to for their people and their program.) Next, he should explain why he needs a specific item and always ask for double the amount he really needs so the procurement officer can laugh like a demon, exercise his power by cutting the request (usually by half), and request his departure. The sniper commander can then express his gratitude and go back to his office feeling smug that he duped the purchasing officer.

If the request is denied, the sniper commander should press for a time when the budget may accommodate his request, go over the requisition weenie's head, go to a more powerful officer, and repeatedly inquire about the equipment requested. If the procurement staff doesn't start cursing when the commander enters the room, he probably isn't going to get his gear.

EQUIPMENT

Sniper team leaders make recommendations for equipment to sniper commanders. This section lists the items snipers need, their usage, and their justification as required for the procurement process.

Primary weapon. The sniper's primary weapon must be capable of subminute of angle accuracy. Many of today's rifles are extremely accurate, so several should be tested prior to making a selection. The most expensive weapon is not always the best, even though price is often indicative of quality. The primary weapon should be individually assigned and maintained.

Secondary weapon. I recommend a suppressed submachine gun or semiauto handgun in case the snipers are compromised prior to the execution phase of an operation.

Match-grade ammunition. Ammunition must be of very high quality and have a very low standard of deviation between rounds. Don't skimp here; a $2,500 rifle can shoot like a $200 rifle if substandard ammo is used. Ammo should be ordered well ahead of time and in bulk so the snipers can work out of the same case lots. Whenever lots are changed, there will usually be a change in aim versus impact.

High-quality rifle scope. The rifle scope should have 1/4-minute adjustments and hand-adjustable turrets that can be both felt and heard. A high level of brightness is necessary as well as duplex or thin crosshairs. The goal here is to be able to identify the target. A good magnification is 12X. This degree of power allows for close shots (20 yards) to be performed as well as long shots (200 yards for the law enforcement sniper). Variable scopes are usually unnecessary, because most snipers leave their scopes on one setting, normally the most powerful. Care must also be taken to ascertain that there are no point-of-aim or point-of-impact shifts as the magnification is adjusted up or down.

Binoculars. Binoculars are handy when moving into position and for panning the tactical area of responsibility. They should be fairly portable, nonreflective, and of high magnification.

Spotting scope. A spotting scope is used from the firing position to pan or zoom into the target area. It should be of high magnification, low profile, nonreflective, and it should have a stable platform.

Night vision device. For observation, get a new-generation night vision device that won't bleach, starburst, or flower out because of artificial lighting sources.

Rifle data book or dope book. The data book contains a complete record of every shot fired through the weapon. It should note the weather conditions, effects of weather on the shooter and equipment, type of rounds used, and information for correct zero at different ranges. These books are commercially available, but to save money you can copy them and tailor them to fit specific needs. Always keep the most current book with the rifle, and never throw old ones away.

Rifle maintenance gear. To correctly maintain their rifles, snipers must carry patches, a cleaning cloth, bore cleaner, a bore brush, gun grease, gun oil, a camel hair brush (for lenses), a bristle paintbrush, a toothbrush, a cleaning rod (one-piece, steel, plastic-coated, rotating-handle type), lens paper, and a rod jag and eye.

Alice pack. This must be large and camouflaged to fit the area of operations. As you can see, there is quite a bit of equipment to carry, and this pack works well.

Tactical vest or web gear. These can be used for carrying items that are used frequently or when on the move.

Camouflage poncho with liner. This is used for protection from rain, wind, cold, and detection while recording information at night or smoking.

Inclement-weather clothing. I can't think of anything that will affect your effectiveness more quickly than inclement weather. It won't do you any good to deploy if you can't survive the weather conditions. Snipers should have Gore-Tex jackets, pants, gloves, and socks, a Nomex hood, and insulated boots. Always get a weather report prior to deployment, and be prepared for drastic weather changes.

Elbow/Knee pads. Elbow and knee pads are used for crawling or lying on hard, rough, cold, or hot surfaces.

Penlight with red lens, compass, large knife, and Leatherman-type tool. The red lens preserves night vision; the compass is for operations on rural terrain; the knife and Leatherman-type tool are used in a variety of situations.

Pencil, paper, notebook, and map. These are to be packaged in plastic wrapping.

Water canteen. This should have a 2-quart capacity and a carrier. It should be made of plastic because it makes less noise. Canteens are available in a variety or camouflage colors.

Food. Food is necessary for operations that may be prolonged. Meals, Ready to Eat (MRE) military rations are probably the easiest and most complete. Taste and selection are not a consideration.

Appropriate hide material. Use camouflage paste, cream, or stick with built-in insect repellent. Earth-tone burlap or ghillie suits are useful in a few specific circumstances. Dyed cheesecloth can be draped in front of the sniper's position or behind to break up backlighting.

Appropriate camouflage uniforms. Stay away from solid colors, especially SWAT black. All these do is silhouette the human body.

Shooting mat. This will insulate snipers from cold, heat, or uncomfortable terrain.

Radio. The radio should have handset, encrypted, and multichannel features. Hands-free operation and capability for ear speakers, boom mikes, and throat mikes are pluses, but keep in mind that ear speakers hurt after awhile and can cause infections, boom mikes can get in the way, and throat mikes can pick up interference such as breathing from exertion. Experiment first, then buy. Always carry two spare batteries in case the deployment is prolonged.

Wristwatch. A sniper's watch should be the luminous hands-type only and have no hourly chime.

Devices to mark your position for emergency purposes. Smoke grenades, strobe lights, or chemical light sticks can be used.

Range finder. This can be complex and expensive or simple and cost-effective. Remember, test it first, then buy. Rifle scopes with mil dots can be used to estimate range.

• • • • •

This list is not all-inclusive and must be tailored to fit each situation. Keep in mind that just because specific SWAT gear is depicted in movies or on TV shows or looks "bitchin'" is not reason to buy it. The measure of any piece of equipment should be how it performs, not how it looks.

CHAPTER TWO

CHAIN OF COMMAND AND DUTIES

O peration orders in various tactical operations are approved in the emergency operations center (EOC). The EOC also provides support and guidance and can set constraints, but it is not a command and control element. It exists to support the tactical operations center (TOC) with logistics and to interface with upper-level parent organization players and other assets. The TOC is the central location for all tactical information to support missions. It depends on other sources for its data, i.e., from witnesses and released hostages, sniper team information, crisis negotiations, technical surveillance, investigative follow-up information, etc. The TOC is designed to capture, fuse, and disseminate information to operational entities. It also supports investigative needs and operational planning. A poor EOC is one that interferes with and attempts to control the TOC's activities. If it wants to do this, and many do, it doesn't believe or trust its tactical operators. Unfortunately, the TOC spends a great deal of time serving as a buffer between the

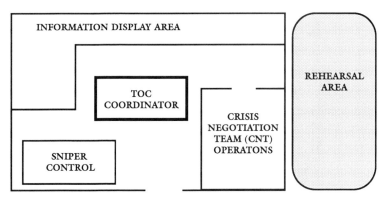

Figure 1: TOC setup.

SWAT team and the EOC distraction. A good TOC commander must possess great political skill to occupy the EOC personnel's attention so the teams can operate.

The TOC is set up a safe distance from the crisis site and is secure and out of the public eye, but it must be close to crisis negotiation team operations and the assault team rehearsal sites. A guard should be placed at the TOC door to prevent the entry of unauthorized personnel. An access roster is helpful for this purpose.

SNIPER CONTROL AREA

The sniper commander runs the sniper control area of the TOC. The following is a list of supplies and information that are gathered and made available in the sniper control area.

Two information recorders
Radios
Phones
Location of target (physical address)
Target photos—aerial, ground, top, and elevated views
Maps of target area, including surrounding area, perimeter control points, danger areas, and obstacles
Biographical information on adversaries
Biographical information on hostages
Demands/Deadline log
Weapons/Explosives
Light/Weather data
Environmental safety precautions and health considerations
Sniper positions
Sniper fields of view
Sniper fields of fire
Sniper call signs
Plotting of sniper movement and setup
Sector sketch, including avenues of approach, avenues of escape, dead space, distance to target, and overlapping fields of fire
Suspect pattern analysis
Target numbering and assignments

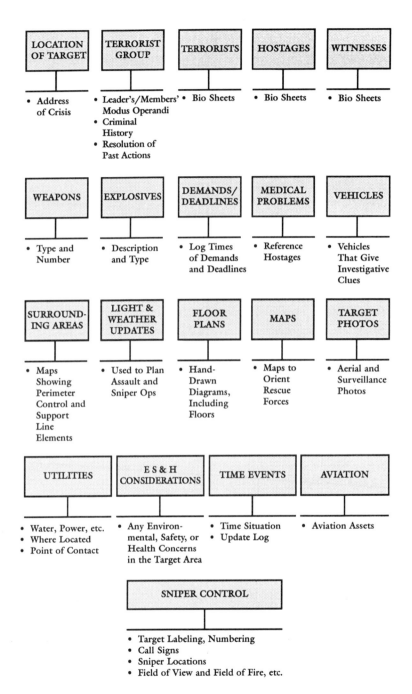

LOCATION OF TARGET	TERRORIST GROUP	TERRORISTS	HOSTAGES	WITNESSES
• Address of Crisis	• Leader's/Members' Modus Operandi • Criminal History • Resolution of Past Actions	• Bio Sheets	• Bio Sheets	• Bio Sheets

WEAPONS	EXPLOSIVES	DEMANDS/ DEADLINES	MEDICAL PROBLEMS	VEHICLES
• Type and Number	• Description and Type	• Log Times of Demands and Deadlines	• Reference Hostages	• Vehicles That Give Investigative Clues

SURROUNDING AREAS	LIGHT & WEATHER UPDATES	FLOOR PLANS	MAPS	TARGET PHOTOS
• Maps Showing Perimeter Control and Support Line Elements	• Used to Plan Assault and Sniper Ops	• Hand-Drawn Diagrams, Including Floors	• Maps to Orient Rescue Forces	• Aerial and Surveillance Photos

UTILITIES	E S & H CONSIDERATIONS	TIME EVENTS	AVIATION
• Water, Power, etc. • Where Located • Point of Contact	• Any Environmental, Safety, or Health Concerns in the Target Area	• Time Situation • Update Log	• Aviation Assets

SNIPER CONTROL

- Target Labeling, Numbering
- Call Signs
- Sniper Locations
- Field of View and Field of Fire, etc.

Figure 2: Sniper control area information display.

Chain of Command and Duties

SNIPER COMMANDER DUTIES

The sniper commander is responsible for the upchanneling and downchanneling of all information requested from the sniper teams. The sniper commander's duties are to gather, compile, and disseminate information to operational entities and assign fields of fire to the sniper teams. He supports the teams' needs and is responsible for procurement, training, deployment, logistics, and deadly-force policy (DFP) constraints. He also decides target numbering and assignments, and runs interference with the other TOC entities.

Diagramming Buildings

Buildings must be diagrammed in a consistent form. For example, label the sides in a clockwise direction, openings from left to right, and levels from bottom to top. The starting point should be the side containing the main entrance/exit point to the building, usually the front door. However, another side can be chosen at the discretion of the sniper commander. This is not a problem as long as all sniper teams and the sniper team leader are aware of it prior to deployment.

There are three systems for labeling buildings: numeric, alphabetical, and color-coded. Mixing methods is also acceptable. Figure 3 illustrates a numerically labeled building, Figure 4 shows a building labeled using an alphabetical system, and Figure 5 illustrates a color-coded method.

If there is a basement, it should be labeled as level one or basement. If there is a penthouse, the same rule applies— label it as another level or as penthouse. If the building is circular, it is best to label it clockwise and divide the building into sections. Odd-shaped buildings can cause some confusion, so plan ahead. As long as all concerned know the labeling procedure, there shouldn't be any problem.

Dead Space

The sniper commander briefs the sniper team leader, who then informs the sniper teams of the dead space in the target

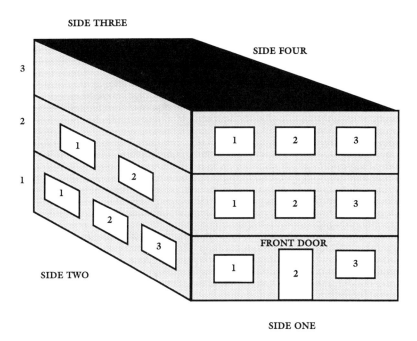

Figure 3: Numerically labeled building. Number the sides in a clockwise direction using the front door as a reference point. Number the openings from left to right. Number the floors from bottom to top.

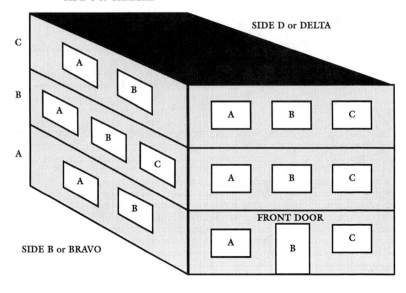

SIDE C or CHARLIE

SIDE D or DELTA

SIDE B or BRAVO

SIDE A or ALPHA

Figure 4: Alphabetically labeled target. The only difference between this figure and Figure 3 is the substitution of letters for numbers.

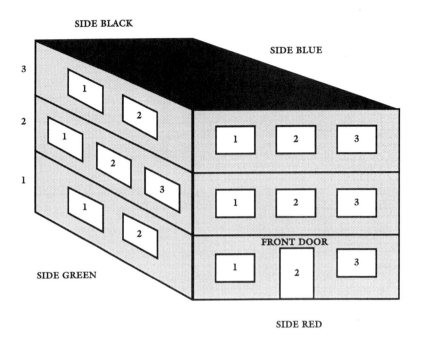

Figure 5: Color-coded labeled target. The difference between this figure and Figures 3 and 4 is the substitution of colors for numbers or letters.

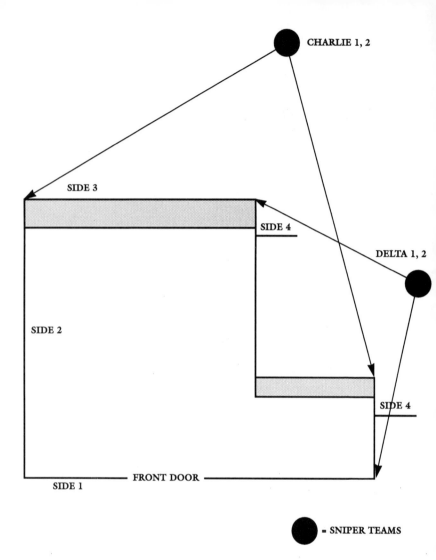

Figure 6: Odd-shaped building labeling (top view). The shaded area illustrates the field of view for Charlie team. As you can see, part of Charlie team's field of view is located on Delta team's side. However, Delta team cannot see this area, so it is Charlie team's responsibility. Sometimes these areas can be viewed after a shift in position is conducted, but in this case this would only cause a loss of view in other locations.

area. For example, snipers are set up in an industrial complex, and one of the rooms to which they have been assigned contains a tank of highly explosive substances. If this tank is punctured, a devastating explosion will result. The EOC decides that shooting in this area is not worth the risk, so the area is marked a "no-shoot area" (dead space). The snipers diagram this information on their range cards so it is available at a glance.

Suspect Pattern Analysis

The sniper commander formulates a suspect pattern analysis as adversaries are observed. For example, at 1300 hours, Alpha team reports, "On side one, level one, opening two, one white male, 6 feet tall, 190 pounds, with brown hair, a beard, wearing sunglasses, a black watch cap, brown coat, blue shirt, blue jeans, white gym shoes, holding a semiauto handgun in his right hand, looks out of opening for 10 seconds." At 1330 hours and again at 1400 hours, Alpha team reports the same information. A pattern has appeared here indicating a possible predictable target area. A plan may be developed to either neutralize the adversary here or avoid this area five minutes before or after the half hour if an assault team is to pass this area or enter this particular opening to lessen the chance of its being discovered by the adversary.

Target Identification, Numbering, and Assignment

Along with the suspect pattern analysis, the sniper commander will try to determine the number of adversaries and hostages, and the identities of each, and will ultimately number and assign targets. The sniper commander feeds the TOC tactical display information and gathers specific adversary and hostage information as other sources report.

If ample information is accumulated in the TOC, sniper teams will be assigned a numbered adversary. As the adversary appears over time and all identifying features match up, the sniper commander will label him as target #1. This enables the team to shorten its reporting and recording procedures.

For example, before the target is numbered, Alpha team would report, "At 1500 hours, side one, level one, opening three, one Caucasian male, 30 years old, 6 feet tall, 190 pounds, brown hair, wearing a red hat, white T-shirt, blue jeans, white gym shoes, and a gold watch on his left wrist, and carrying a semiauto handgun in his right hand, looked outside for 10 seconds." The subsequent radio transmission would be, "At 1700 hours, side one, level one, opening three, target #1 looked outside for 10 seconds."

It is important that any changes in the information on the adversary be reported. If a consistent description does not develop, target labeling cannot be accomplished. One section of the suspect identification report that is of particular interest in the TOC is the distinguishing characteristics portion. This consists of identifying aspects of the adversary, such as scars, tattoos, eyeglasses, beard, mustache, hair length, watch, rings, necklaces, physical deformities, etc. Many times adversaries exchange clothes with each other or hostages and try disguises, but they usually forget to remove or change jewelry. So, if three differently dressed adversaries are observed, but all are wearing the same watch, ring, and necklace, chances are it is the same person. The sniper must never use clothing as the basis for an identifiable target when making a shot.

As the situation unfolds over time, the sniper commander may procure pictures of adversaries and hostages from the TOC information pool. He will then assign target numbers to the adversaries' photographs and include some information that the suspect pattern analysis has revealed. These pictures will be hand-delivered to each sniper in each position by the sniper team leader. Numbering and the utilization of numbering are now complete.

In the identification reports, the adversary, or target, is depersonalized and the hostage is personalized. The depersonalization is done in an effort to make the shot as mechanical as possible. If the targets can't be numbered by identity because of lack of time or information, the sniper team leader will use a field-expedient method. Using this method, targets

SWAT Sniper: Deployment and Control

16

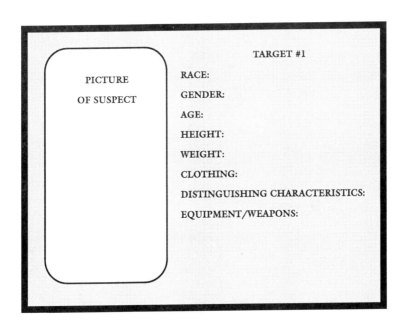

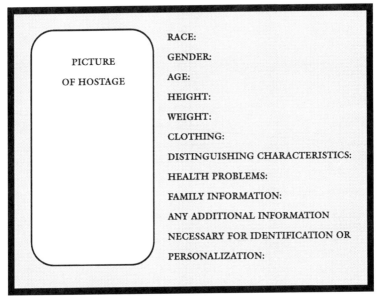

Figure 7: Target and hostage identification reports.

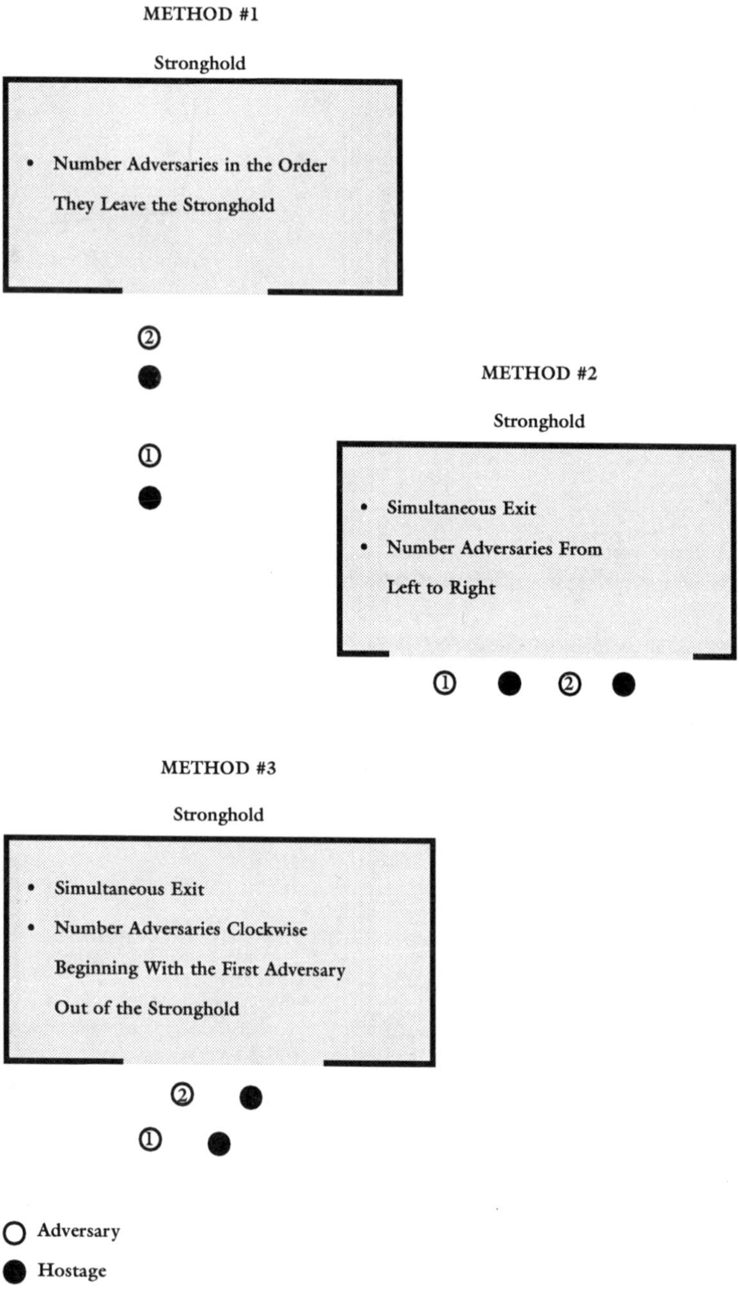

METHOD #1

Stronghold

- Number Adversaries in the Order
  They Leave the Stronghold

② ●

① ●

METHOD #2

Stronghold

- Simultaneous Exit
- Number Adversaries From
  Left to Right

① ● ② ●

METHOD #3

Stronghold

- Simultaneous Exit
- Number Adversaries Clockwise
  Beginning With the First Adversary
  Out of the Stronghold

② ●
① ●

O Adversary
● Hostage

Figure 8: Target numbering by field-expedient method.

are assigned in the order in which they leave the stronghold, or, if a simultaneous exit transpires, they are numbered from left to right or clockwise.

The field-expedient method leaves ample room for error, not of identification but of insufficient sniper coverage. The sniper-to-adversary ratio should be two to one (2:1). Two snipers are assigned to each adversary for shot assurance.

Although the field-expedient method is not nearly as efficient as deliberate target assignment, it enables the open-air assault (sniper neutralization) to be used in a rapidly unfolding scenario. Target assignments do not negate or change the department's DFP. They are only used to coordinate fire on targets. The sniper ultimately decides if he is going to shoot or not. This constraint illustrates the importance of the 2:1 ratio—if one sniper can't shoot, the other should be able to.

SNIPER TEAM LEADER DUTIES

The sniper team leader prepares and briefs sniper teams; deploys and monitors sniper team progress; approves sniper team positions; reviews sniper team range cards for proper building labeling, field of view, and field of fire information; monitors sniper team radio transmissions for accurate, clear, concise, complete, and timely information; checks the status of the sniper teams as required and disseminates TOC information to them; and ensures that changes in position are completed as required.

The sniper team leader functions in coordination and cooperation with the sniper control area. Through continuous situation updates, the sniper commander and team leader will formulate final firing positions and order the teams to shift to an area that enables them to observe the predictable target area. The sniper team leader strives for the 2:1 sniper-to-adversary ratio, which requires clear fields of view and overlapping fields of fire. The sniper positions at this point must be mutually supporting.

The sniper team leader formulates a sketch (sector sketch)

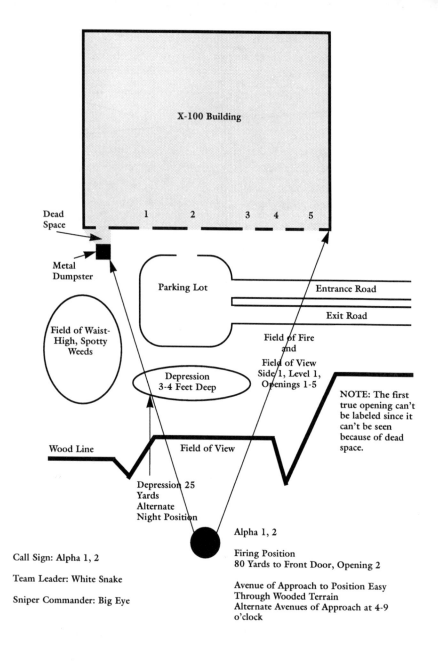

Figure 9: Range card information.

of the complete sniper team deployment by copying and compiling the snipers' range cards. Range cards are used in the field as a ready reference for information and to refresh the team's memory in case a relief team arrives. Range cards contain information pertaining to the distance from the firing position to the target, field of view, field of fire (when assigned), dead space, alternate positions, and call signs.

The sector sketch is plotted in the sniper control area. The sniper team leader is also responsible for giving the actual fire commands. He supervises the withdrawal of the sniper teams and performs a debriefing upon completion of the mission.

The sniper team leader should never allow his snipers to be used as containment forces. If this is done, the snipers' utilization is severely restricted as the situation develops. Nontactical officers should always maintain the cordon controlling personnel and traffic and preventing the adversary from escaping.

Phase Lines

The sniper team leader establishes phase lines in conjunction with the sniper teams. Phase lines can be color-coded, alphabetical, or numerical.

The proper use of phase lines can be illustrated using Alpha team and color-coded phase lines. For instance, Alpha team has been directed to set up on side one of X-100 building. Before the team members are deployed, their course should be plotted, beginning with their line of departure (LOD), or starting point, which should be close to the TOC but not the TOC proper. Radio transmissions between Alpha team and the sniper commander in the sniper control area are as follows:

Alpha team: Alpha team to Big Eye, over.
Sniper commander: Go ahead Alpha team, over.
Alpha team: Have initiated phase line black, over.
Sniper commander: Copy black, over.

(The TOC plots the team's location.)

Chain of Command and Duties

Alpha team: Alpha team to Big Eye, over.
Sniper commander: Go ahead Alpha team, over.
Alpha team: Have completed phase line black, initiate blue.
Sniper commander: Copy blue, over.

(The TOC plots the team's location.)

Alpha team: Alpha team to Big Eye, over.
Sniper commander: Go ahead Alpha team, over
Alpha team: Have completed phase line blue, initiate yellow.
Sniper commander: Copy yellow, over.

(The TOC plots the team's location.)

These transmissions continue until Alpha team reaches its final firing position in building X-14, when it will transmit, "Have completed phase line red, in place 100 yards, side one, clear field of view." The TOC will plot the team's location, and the sniper commander will respond, "Copy 100 yards, side one, all clear, out."

Even if the radio is compromised by adversaries, the news media, or the curious, these transmissions tell them nothing. In keeping with this idea, snipers must never give their position by direction, i.e., north, south, east, or west. For example, in lieu of transmitting "100 yards, side one, clear field of view," adversaries would hear "100 yards, south side of building X-100, clear field of view," which compromises the snipers' position. In addition, the word sniper should never be used on the open network, because it is a media magnet.

Phase lines also allow the sniper teams to give ready status reports without long, nebulous radio transmissions, so the sniper commander is ready when the EOC wants a situation report. If a team gets into trouble, the team leader can readily find its location. He will also follow the team's route of travel when shagging their positions throughout the mission.

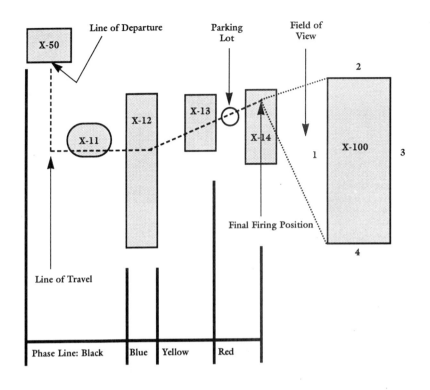

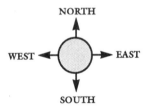

Figure 10: Color-coded phase lines. Phase line black begins at the west side of building X-50 and ends at the west side of building X-12. Phase line blue begins at the west side of building X-12 and ends at the east side of building X-12. Phase line yellow begins at the east side of building X-12 and ends at the east side of building X-13. Phase line red begins at the east side of building X-13 and ends at the final firing position in building X-14.

Chain of Command and Duties

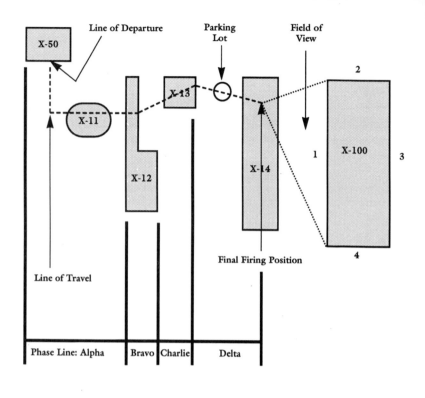

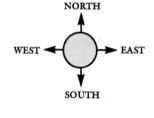

Figure 11: Phonetic alphabet phase lines. Phase line Alpha begins at the west side of building X-50 and ends at the west side of building X-12. Phase line Bravo begins at the west side of building X-12 and ends at the east side of building X-12. Phase line Charlie begins at the east side of building X-12 and ends at the east side of building X-13. Phase line Delta begins at the east side of building X-13 and ends at the final firing position in building X-14.

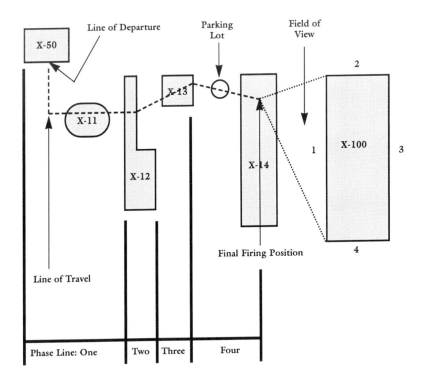

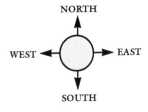

Figure 12: Numeric phase lines. Phase line one begins at the west side of building X-50 and ends at the west side of building X-12. Phase line two begins at the west side of building X-12 and ends at the east side of building X-12. Phase line three begins at the east side of building X-12 and ends at the east side of building X-13. Phase line four begins at the east side of building X-13 and ends at the final firing position in building X-14.

Sniper Team Positioning

The sniper team leader chooses the sniper teams' positions in the target area. He may choose to use either a 360-degree deployment as depicted in Figure 13 or diagonal configuration shown in Figure 14. The ultimate configuration is the 360-degree coverage, but this deployment is subject to manpower and time constraints, as well as the uniqueness of the target area.

Fire Commands

To coordinate sniper shots, fire commands are transmitted by radio and should be backed up with an additional sound or visual effect. The sniper team leader should carry two radios and two extra batteries for each radio. The fire commands are as follows:

STAND BY—Shooters look through their scopes at the target.

READY—Shooters take their safeties off, rest their fingers on the trigger, then track, ambush, or track and hold their targets. The sniper team leader initiates this command as the target comes into view.

(The STAND BY and READY commands are given in a monotone voice, but the FIRE command is emphasized.)

FIRE—Rounds out.

The time span between the READY and FIRE commands must be very short. If not, bring the shooters down. The DOWN sequence is as follows.

STAND BY: Same as above.
READY: Same as above.

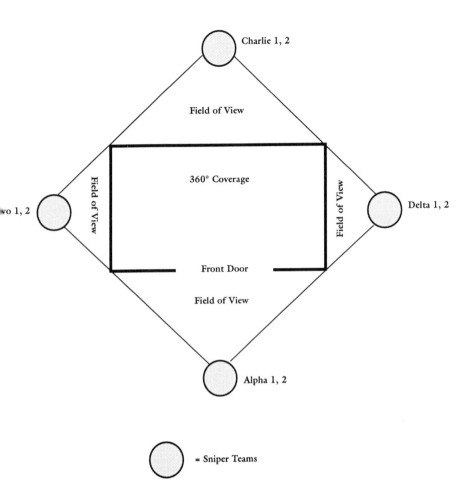

Figure 13: 360-degree deployment. Each team is responsible for one side.

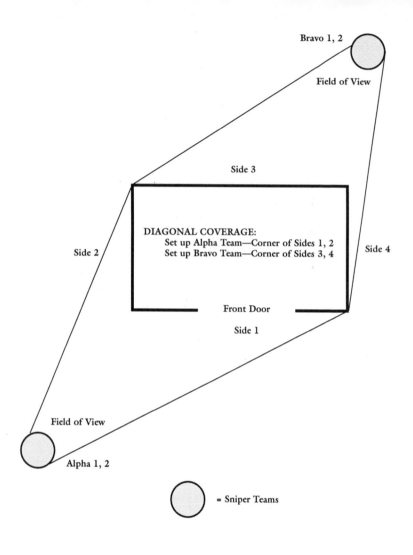

Figure 14: Diagonal deployment. Diagonal deployment is set up on opposite corners of a building. This figure depicts a 1, 2 corner setup and a 3, 4 corner setup requiring each team to cover two sides. Coverage is weak, and snipers have poor fields of view because of angles and window glare.

(The sniper team leader should wait about 30 seconds from the READY command before giving the DOWN command. If he waits, the snipers will realize they are coming down. This command should be said in a monotone voice, and the word should be elongated, i.e., "doowwn.")

DOWN: Fingers come off the trigger, and safeties go back on. The snipers go back to STAND BY mode.

The FIRE command should be backed up with another sound. Distraction devices with 1- to 1 1/2-second fuses are good for this purpose. If the communications net goes down, the distraction device will serve as the FIRE command. The commands would be as follows:

STAND BY
READY
FIRE (simultaneously throw device)

Another fire command system is the countdown, for which the commands are as follows:

STAND BY
READY
5, 4, 3, 2, 1, FIRE

If the DOWN command is necessary when using the countdown command system, the sniper team leader should cease the countdown, wait a few seconds, and then give the DOWN command. Two situations in which the countdown command is useful are the night shot and the window shot. The following commands are for a night shot.

STAND BY
READY
5, 4, 3, 2 (lights illuminate target), 1, FIRE

For a window shot, the commands are the following:

STAND BY
READY
5, 4, 3, 2 (first sniper fires to break the glass), 1, FIRE
(second sniper engages target)

The window glass is broken first to ensure a clear shot on target. Windows can cause ricochets, deflections, secondary high-speed fragments, and clear misses. Internal and external ballistics can be predicted, but not terminal ballistics. Once the bullet is upset, it may go anywhere.

The purpose of the fire command sequence is to avoid premature or delayed shots. Premature shots can warn adversaries, miss, cause a reaction by hostages (panic), distract other snipers (cause them to fire or not fire), allow unharmed adversaries to kill hostages, or cause vehicle and building assault teams to initiate prematurely. Delayed shots do the same but also endanger assault teams that are moving into the snipers' field of fire. Follow-up shots should be used sparingly, and snipers must never shoot into the stronghold once assault teams have entered.

After shots are fired, each sniper will radio "round out, one suspect down," or whatever the target status is, and continue to observe until the assault team clears the area.

Command and Control

If the EOC approves an open-air assault, command and control passes from the sniper commander to the sniper team leader. This usually happens after a predictable target area has been established. Can command and control revert back to the commander? Yes, if the open-air assault is delayed or canceled, which is not unusual as negotiations proceed or stall.

But these delays can be helpful because they enable planning and rehearsals to continue, and a nontactical solution may be ultimately achieved.

CHAPTER THREE

SNIPER TEAM DUTIES

The common perception of a sniper is as a lone officer who is lean and mean, very quiet, has deep, penetrating eyes, is the best rifle shot in the department, and carries a death ace in his pocket. He is called out, he sets up, shoots once, carves a notch in his stock, packs up, and then goes home. This notion is a considerable sack of fecal matter. It is a gross misrepresentation. Sadly, many departments misuse and underuse their sniper teams because of these misconceptions. The real qualities to look for in snipers are interest, self-reliance, trainability, adaptability, physical fitness, emotional stability, maturity, intelligence, and motivation.

Each sniper team is made up of two men who are equally equipped and trained. Why two men? In any call-out, the time on target is indeterminate. Missions can last from a few hours to days. How can one man sitting in position requiring heightened vigilance for hours on end record, report, communicate, observe, and then shoot at a moment's notice? Surprisingly, some departments have one designated sniper and believe they are in good shape, but their sniper capability is in name only.

The sniper team effort begins with each team member helping the other prepare for the call-out. This includes taking notes at the briefing, checking gear, camouflaging each other, using sound tactical principles while moving to the target, setting up, and sharing duties: one observing and one resting, one observing and one recording, one reporting and one observing, one providing security and one shooting, or both shooting in a multiple-target scenario. These duties require the snipers to have equal training and equipment.

In the past, sniper teams were called sniper-observer teams

and consisted of one shooter and one observer. This is a 50-percent waste of manpower. Why arm only one sniper when you already have two set up? It is for this same reason that snipers should not share a rifle. Not only does sharing a rifle reduce the team's strength by 50 percent, it is dangerous. The sniper rifle is a precision instrument tuned to a specific shooter. The main problem with sharing a rifle is eye relief, or the distance that the back of the scope is set from the shooter's eye in relation to the spot weld on the stock. This means one shooter will be playing catch-up by either craning or crunching his neck to negate the black moons. Black moons are shadows in the scope resulting from poor eye relief or eye position, which causes the shot to go in the opposite direction of the moons. Depending on how the shooter compensates, he may make the shot, but if he is too far forward, he may sustain a "magnum eyebrow," a nice half-moon cut above the eye caused when the scope recoils. Many times this cut requires sutures and results in a bad case of flinching. If he is too far back, he may make a peripheral hit, miss entirely, or hit an innocent party. Why take the chance? The idea is precision, not to fire into a crowd and hope for the best.

Sniper team duties, other than neutralization of adversaries, include providing high ground or low-level cover for 1) negotiators; 2) personnel delivering food, phones, or whatever is granted during negotiations; 3) hostages who are being recovered; and 4) assault teams moving into position. Sniper teams gather information about their field of view and position, and provide adversary and hostage updates. They also report movement, physical descriptions, and weapons for suspect and hostage pattern analyses. Finally, they can neutralize adversaries when appropriate and either end the problem or decrease the load the assault team is responsible for by cutting the strength of a group of adversaries. But the most overlooked and underused sniper duty is scouting or reconnaissance (recon). Snipers are the eyes and ears of the TOC as well as of the SWAT team. Don't get confused here; the snipers are part of the SWAT team, but when assigned sniper duties, they become a separate entity. When not used as snipers, they are integrated back into the SWAT team. This necessitates cross-training.

SCOUTING DUTIES

Snipers scout the terrain from the TOC to the target to get an accurate time frame for the maneuver. The assault team then uses the time frame (time hack) in their scheme of maneuver instead of estimating. Yes, there will still be a plus (fat) or minus (lean) factor, but the assault window will be much more accurate. Sometimes the teams arrive on target too soon or race in disarray to catch up. Since the SWAT team is operating in a permissive hostile environment from the time it leaves the TOC to the completion of its mission, a lean time hack is much worse than a fat time hack, which can be adjusted for en route. I have seen teams run to the target, set up, and insert with no rest on a lean time hack. This may not sound bad unless you had to run in full gear, possibly wearing a protective mask, and had to account for team members, thus sacrificing security for speed, all while rehearsing your duties in your mind. Believe me, in such situations the suck factor is high, and your fun meter is pegged out!

TERRAIN ANALYSIS

The sniper team can also provide a terrain analysis. It will evaluate the terrain for key features, avenues of approach and escape, obstacles, observation points, cover, concealment, and danger areas. An example of a key feature is high ground. Does the adversary have this advantage, and if not, can the sniper team or SWAT team use it? Does the adversary have clear fields of fire over possible avenues of approach? The hard way to find this out is to deploy blind and wing it. Instead, the sniper team should report its findings to the sniper control area, and plans should be devised accordingly.

Avenues of Approach

Two or more avenues of approach to the target should be planned in the event one or more is compromised. Depending on sniper team strength, the bare minimum deployment is two two-man teams (four snipers) dispersed diagonally on opposite corners of a building. The optimum is four two-man teams (eight snipers) positioned 360 degrees around the building. After the snipers cross the terrain, they know the fastest route, safest route, easiest route, and most dangerous route. SWAT teams plug this information into their tactical constraints and then determine which route to take according to whether they are hurting for time (the speed versus security option), they have time (security versus speed option), or these options combine to acceptable tactical degrees. SWAT teams work in an unpredictable, fluid environment where the situation dictates their plans. Sniper teams are their tools for evaluating that environment.

Obstacles

The SWAT teams may encounter obstacles during their approach. For example, the time hack is on the mark, and the SWAT team is five minutes from the assault point when it encounters an 8-foot-high chain-link fence topped with barbed wire. Its options are to either choose an alternate route or breach the fence. Both are time-consuming, and the team is hanging out in that damn permissive tactical environment. Of course, you know the team has bolt cutters to snip the fence, right? (And I have a Batman utility belt that neutralizes any situation.) The point is that there are incalculable obstacles to be breached or circumvented in any tactical arena, and team leaders can't predict them all.

The sniper teams can report these obstacles, so when the SWAT team leader asks the sniper control area for a terrain analysis and two avenues of approach, he can choose a route that facilitates a speedy, concealed approach. Before deploying, however, he may be informed of a fence obstacle. Instead of getting caught in the above dog knot, he can plan on having bolt cutters and a tactical formation for security purposes, order of movement, and regrouping. He can also plan whether or not the SWAT team will leave the bolt cutters behind.

Danger Areas

Another tactical consideration the sniper teams note is any danger areas. Danger areas include any obstacle, terrain feature, or area that may subject the SWAT team to fire or compromise. There is considerable danger involved in something as simple as breaching a fence. If unplanned, and events go to hell in a hand basket, the team can sustain casualties, be split on either side of the fence, be delayed by harassing fire, be neutralized by loss of personnel, deplete ammo, or never make it to the target area. This may cause the whole tactical plan to fail, because the team is part of the overall solution.

Danger areas can heighten the chance of compromise, loss of surprise, or just plain throw the time hack so far out that the mission is finished before it has begun. The sniper team reports these danger areas when asked by the sniper control area, enabling the SWAT team to plan circumvention/breaching techniques, vehicle usage such as tactical trucks, etc.

TARGET RECON

Another sniper team duty is target recon, also an area where the sniper team can assist the SWAT team in tactical planning. Sniper teams can tell SWAT teams

- whether windows are open or closed, lights are on or off, doors are open or closed or padlocked or chained;
- whether there is outside cover or obstructions (parked cars, shrubs, Dumpsters, etc.);
- what footing there is leading to doors or stairs (water, ice, snow, pea gravel, etc.);
- whether there are steps to doors, how many, and whether they break right or left;
- whether the porch is big enough for the whole team;

- the location of outside lights and whether they're on or off, have motion detectors, are timed, etc.;
- where the phone and electric lines and heating vents are;
- whether there are outside access areas (boiler rooms, phone rooms, loading docks, etc.);
- what type of structure it is;
- whether there are any obviously barricaded areas or blank exterior walls; etc.

The sniper team can also take still pictures, run video cameras, and use listening devices and other high-speed, low-drag gear.

OVERWATCH DUTIES

The sniper team can provide cover for other law enforcement personnel involved in activities that expose them to gunfire, such as during the delivery of negotiated items or the maneuvering of assault teams into position. They also cover released hostages. Crisis negotiators who achieve a hostage release can instruct the hostage to walk to a certain area out of the target view and use the sniper team as a snatch team. Snipers can also provide a high level of security at a specific location to deny criminals the opportunity to injure or kill citizens, VIPs, witnesses, or others who may be targeted for assassination.

CHAPTER FOUR

PLANNING THE DEPLOYMENT

O kay, it's a call-out. What happens now? Before the sniper team even musters, there should be an outer cordon and perhaps an inner cordon of line officers. All SWAT operators must contact the field commander to inform him of their impending presence before moving into the area.

While on the mission, sniper team leaders and snipers should try to minimize fatigue, because tired men become careless. They should follow this old military concept: "never stand up when you can sit down, never sit down when you can lie down, never stay awake when you can sleep." If the sniper team leader shows confidence, his team will have confidence. He must never lose his temper, because it will affect his judgment. He must keep cool, think ahead, and always have an alternate plan in mind. And he should not be afraid to take advice from his team members.

ANALYZE THE MISSION

The sniper team leader analyzes the mission to determine who will do what, where, when, and why. He gathers information from witnesses, the field command post commander, and inner and outer cordon officers. Once the sniper team leader has gathered as much essential information as possible, he considers the mission, adversary situation, terrain, weather, time constraints, and available manpower. In assessing the adversary situation, he must determine the type of adversary he is dealing with. Below are some types of adversaries and their behavior.

Mentally disturbed—often has no plan, hard to negotiate with, unpredictable, may be unrealistic.

Terrorist—often has a plan, hard to negotiate with, well organized and equipped; may be very violent, seeking death and destruction.

Criminal—often has no plan; usually has been caught in a criminal act and is trying to bargain; willing to negotiate; predictable.

THE WARNING ORDER

The warning order is prepared by the sniper team leader and is used to warn sniper teams of an impending mission and to organize their preparation. The warning order is an emergency plan that is used in lieu of an operations order because of time and information constraints. It is used in two instances: first, as a prelude to the operations order when immediate action is necessary, and second, to change or adjust to situations or actions already put into motion. The operations order is a full-scale information-dependent plan. It contains much greater detail and requires preparation time ranging from several hours to days.

The detail covered in the warning order is determined by the sniper team leader through his evaluation of the mission profile to ensure proper coverage. He should ask team members to hold all questions until the end of the brief to prevent breaking his chain of thought and deliver the warning order in a clear, concise tone of voice.

The sniper team leader must be prepared to brief other sections participating in the overall mission. (This is usually done by the sniper commander but may fall on the sniper team leader's shoulders.) For example, a building assault team may require a sniper-initiated entry. After the building assault team gives its brief, the sniper team leader will dovetail his with it to ensure coverage and understanding. This meshes the two plans into a completed operations order.

Situation

This is a brief statement of the enemy and friendly situation. It covers the situation, activity, location, parties involved, time, and equipment. For example, the sniper team leader may announce, "On 01/20/95 at 0900, an armed militant group of four to six self-described freedom fighters entered the X-100 administration building located at First and Lincoln Streets. The terrorists are armed with submachine guns, handguns, and explosives. Intelligence is validated by an employee who escaped the initial assault."

Mission

The mission should be tailored to fit the patrol. It covers the following subjects: who, what, when, where, and why. For example, the sniper team leader will say, "Sniper teams will perform full reconnaissance leaving the line of departure (X-50 building adjacent to the TOC) at 1200 hours today, setting up 360-degree positions on the X-100 administration building to report intelligence or neutralize subjects on command."

Who—sniper teams
What—full reconnaissance
When—1200 hours today
Where—X-100 administration building
Why—report intelligence or neutralize subjects

General Instructions

General instructions are the heart of the warning order. Keep in mind that at this point, the sniper teams have very little information to go on. They are the information gatherers for the assault team's operations order. To the best of his ability, the sniper team leader covers the chain of command, general and special organization, individual assignments and responsibilities, specialized equipment required, individual weapon assignments, ammunition considerations, and uniform and equipment common to all. Special instructions are outlined, such as rules of engagement, deadly force policies, compromise procedures, phase lines, communication methods, and fire commands (initial and backup). Time hacks are established for planning and guidance purposes, and the sniper team leader schedules times for initial and final briefs, inspection of individuals and gear, and insertion.

Chain of Command and Call Signs

A chain of command is developed to facilitate the transfer of control to another leader if normal leadership functions break down because of casualties. The chain of command begins with the sniper commander and ends with the last sniper. Call signs are identifiers used when calling someone on the radio. Real names are not normally used in sensitive operations. The following are typical chain of command and call signs used for missions.

Chain of Command	Call Sign
Sniper commander	Big Eye
Sniper team leader	White Snake
Alpha team: 1) Parker	Alpha 1
2) Overly	Alpha 2
Bravo team: 1) Souders	Bravo 1
2) Jindra	Bravo 2
Charlie team: 1) Douglas	Charlie 1
2) Chattin	Charlie 2
Delta team: 1) Schmidt	Delta 1
2) Austerman	Delta 2
Reserve sniper team	Echo

Assignment of Sniper Teams

The sniper team leader assigns each sniper team to set up

in a particular area, such as the side of a building. He should show the sniper teams their assigned areas on a rough sketch and ask the snipers if they understand. These assignments are posted in the briefing area, which can be anywhere near the TOC (a van, a room, an open field, etc.), and a copy is carried by each team. Once the teams are inserted, each will notify the TOC of its location and field of view.

Target Assignment

Target assignment is used to provide proper sniper coverage of adversaries. A general rule is to have two snipers covering each adversary.

Additional Duties, Control Features, and Assets

The teams are also briefed on any additional duties or control features and attached special purpose personnel or additional assets, such as helicopters.

Specialized Equipment

The snipers are instructed to obtain necessary equipment and support items, for example, night vision devices with extra batteries, or photographic equipment. The reserve team can be used for getting the equipment for the snipers.

Uniform and Equipment

The uniform and supplemental equipment to be used are determined by each department. Some examples of supplemental equipment that may be used are bolt cutters, ropes, ladders, grappling hooks, door wedges, glass cutters, etc. The department's standard operating procedure (SOP) should provide a list of standard equipment.

Weapons

The weapons to be used are those that are normally assigned. Upon evaluation of the situation, the sniper team leader may determine if any special weapons are required.

Deadly-Force Policies and Rules of Engagement

Snipers are briefed on departmental deadly-force policies, rules of engagement (ROE), and compromise procedures. The department's DFP, which consists of various judicial and departmental guidelines, should be reiterated so no one thinks that he can deviate from this policy. Rules of engagement are usually restricted versions of the DFP that make normally acceptable rules unacceptable for a particular situation. For example, an ROE may state that the snipers may use deadly force only to protect themselves from serious bodily harm or death.

Normally, when first deployed, the snipers will not be given the option to fire on a suspect at the first opportunity (target of opportunity neutralization). For example: there are multiple hostages and multiple adversaries, and Alpha team observes a hostage being shot in an office. Do the snipers shoot? Consider this first: if they shoot in an attempt to save the hostage, the remaining adversaries may kill as many remaining hostages as they desire. The dilemma here is obvious: save the part and destroy the whole, or sacrifice the part to save the whole. If the snipers haven't been given explicit ROE orders, what will their tendency be? The only way the ROE can be expanded in this case is if there is an emergency entry team ready to assault in the event of compromise or killing. The sniper team leader orders the expansion or limitation of the ROE as the situation necessitates.

The snipers can't be ordered not save their own lives if compromised. This is why I advocate suppressed submachine guns or handguns for snipers to quietly neutralize an adversary who has discovered them and is going to shoot them. Neutralizing the adversary in this situation may buy time until he is discovered.

Compromise Procedures

Snipers must have it ingrained in their minds that they must not be compromised. If the snipers are compromised or discovered, the adversaries may kill hostages, cause catastrophic damage, break off negotiations, or fire into the surrounding tactical arena endangering all nearby personnel and bystanders. Discovery may also cause premature building assaults, panic hostages, or, at a minimum, heighten the adversaries' vigilance. The situation should be analyzed carefully, and the compromise procedure must be tailored to fit possible adversary actions. Here is an example: many times an adversary who is talking to a negotiator will say, "I see a sniper in back of the building." This is usually a probe and shouldn't be taken at face value. Ask the adversary to describe what he sees and get the exact location. If he is correct, the solution could be anything from simple relocation to assault depending on the adversary's actions.

Phase Lines

Phase lines are established so the sniper teams can report their progress to the TOC rapidly and with a minimum of radio traffic.

SALUTE Report

A SALUTE report is an organized, coherent method of reporting activity observed. The layout is as follows:

S—size, how many?
A—activity, what are they doing?
L—location, where are they?
U—uniform, clothing, physical description
T—time observed
E—equipment, weapons, gear

The sniper team leader instructs sniper teams to transmit SALUTE reports at designated times throughout the mission.

Fire Command

The type of fire command to be used during the mission is determined by the sniper team leader. For example, he may announce, "If fire commands are required, they will be deliv-

Planning the Deployment

ered by standard radio command and deployment of a distraction device."

Time Schedule

The time schedule is determined by the sniper team leader and is used to identify critical events. It is posted in the briefing area. For example:

Current time: 1000 hours
Initial brief: 1015 hours
Final brief: 1030 hours
Inspection: 1115 hours
Insertion: 1200 hours

CHAPTER FIVE

Sniper Team Deployment

At this point, the sniper teams have been briefed, inspected, and cleared to leave the line of departure. Their first objective is to avoid being compromised—they must remain undetected throughout the operation. Snipers must remain alert and aware of their surroundings from the time they depart on a mission until the time they return.

TARGET INDICATORS

To avoid compromise, the snipers must be aware of target indicators: things the adversary will be looking for to detect their presence.

Sound

The first indicator is sound, which can be made by people moving around, rattling equipment, or talking. The adversary might dismiss certain noises as those that belong in the setting, but the human voice is a dead giveaway. To communicate during the mission, snipers should make maximum use of hand and arm signals. They should also be aware of the effects that the time of day and weather conditions have on sound. For example, noise travels much farther on clear, cold nights than on overcast nights with drizzling rain. The reason for this is reduced ambient noise and enhanced hearing at night. If there is ambient noise in the area, snipers should make use of it when moving. For instance, they should move faster when an aircraft passes overhead or when traffic passes by. Before deploying on a mission, gear should be silenced by taping it down so that it makes no noise while running or walking. To move quietly, snipers should use slow, deliberate, smooth movements.

Movement

Movement itself is an indicator because the human eye is naturally attracted to it. A stationary object may be impossible to detect, and a slow-moving one might be left unnoticed, but one moving with quick, jerky movements will definitely attract attention.

Reflection

Snipers must also be aware of reflection from shiny objects that are exposed and not toned down, such as belt buckles, watches, jewelry, ammunition, and eyeglasses. Even the lenses of optical gear can reflect light. Sunshades and shadows should be used whenever possible.

Outlines

The outlines of objects such as the body, head, shoulders, weapons, and other gear can be very recognizable from a distance. The human eye will often pick up a recognizable shape and concentrate on it even if the object cannot be identified right away. All outlines must be broken up into indistinguishable patterns.

Background

The snipers must blend in with the background, not stand out against it. When moving, observing, or choosing a position, they must look for backgrounds that will conceal the coloring and shape of their bodies and gear. Also, snipers must not backlight themselves by walking upright on roofs or hilltops. They should stay in the shadows as much as possible and walk through buildings, if possible, instead of around them.

Distractions

Deceptions and distractions can be used to help the snipers move into position. For example, a policeman can be talking on a bullhorn on the opposite side of the target area so the adversary looks in that direction while the snipers move into their positions in the target area.

Camouflage

Before operating in an area, the snipers should study the terrain, vegetation, and lay of the land in the target area to determine the best type of camouflage to use. They must be aware that no one type of camouflage can be used in all terrain or during all seasons. Therefore, they should wear appropriate uniforms and face paint and freshen camouflage as necessary.

The snipers must be conscious of the changes in vegetation, terrain features, and manmade objects as they proceed through the area and make use of the shadows, cover, and concealment these objects provide. But regardless of how well camouflaged the snipers are, they must keep in mind that camouflage techniques do not make them invisible and are not a substitute for sound tactical movement and a well-planned route.

STALKING

The object of stalking is to enable the snipers to move unseen into a firing position and within such range of their target that they are sure of first-round accuracy. The exact location of the target area should be memorized, noting features and landmarks, and the best line of advance should be selected and divided into phase lines. The type of movement likely to be used in each phase line should be considered to help with planning time hacks. Alternate routes should be planned in case the primary route is compromised even though it is difficult to change routes once the snipers are committed to one.

The snipers should move into position using sound tactical movement principles and set up as close to the target area as possible. After all, why should they settle for a 100-yard shot if they can make a 75-yard shot? During the stalk, they should always move as a team—one man moves while one man covers—and take advantage of natural cover and dead space. The snipers should try to avoid animals, which if disturbed may draw attention to their position, and they should take advantage of local disturbances and distractions that may enable them to move a little faster than normal. Also, if the snipers know they can't be observed by the adversary, they should take advantage of it and move rapidly; they shouldn't crawl if they can walk, because crawling is very slow and physically taxing.

As the snipers advance, they should consider each phase line in greater detail, noting the position and frequency of obstacles, the location of known or possible adversary positions, and likely points from which observations can be made. They should try to coordinate their observation points with the beginnings and endings of their phase lines, and when they reach these points, they should observe frequently and maintain their camouflage. To keep themselves oriented, they can use a compass, a wristwatch, or a terrain countdown. The terrain countdown is done by mentally checking off prominent terrain and man-made features that were noted during planning.

If the snipers are surprised or exposed, they must act immediately. They may choose to freeze, move quickly to the nearest cover, or institute planned compromise procedures.

CHOOSING THE FIRING POSITION

Upon arrival in the target area, the sniper team must select their observation/firing position in the configuration chosen by the sniper team leader (360-degree or diagonal). The team should look for a position that offers the optimum balance between maximum fields of fire and maximum cover and concealment. The choices range from positions with natural concealment, such as grass, bushes, shadows, ravines, hollows, and reverse slopes, to positions where cover is provided by man-made structures, such as tunnels or buildings. The sniper must avoid positions that are obvious to the adversary, such as a lone building, single tree, or prominent terrain feature.

OCCUPYING THE FIRING POSITION

The snipers should not take a position just because it is convenient. When the situation permits, they may have to construct and use alternate positions to cover an area effectively. Careful consideration must be given to the route into and out of the position. A worn path can be easily detected. The route should be concealed, and, if possible, covered. This is very important to the sniper team leader, who will be shagging their positions, or for possible relief snipers. Different positions may be used at night or when a predictable target area has been established.

Selecting a well-covered and concealed firing position is not guarantee of the snipers' safety. They must assume that their position is under adversary observation at all times and observe safety precautions. Whenever possible, they should choose a position that has a terrain obstacle between them and the target. This prevents or delays an adversary who may probe their position and expands their options to freeze, move, or employ compromise procedures.

Once in position, one of the snipers performs a hasty search in order to identify any immediate threat. First, he quickly scans back and forth with his eyes in overlapping bands from their position out to approximately 50 yards. Anything suspicious should be examined with optics, and the other team member should use binoculars and do the same thing. They should not rearrange the foliage to better conceal their position while observing and, instead, observe through the vegetation using their optics. Next, a slow, deliberate search is done with optics in overlapping 180-degree arc patterns from the position to any distance deemed necessary. The snipers should observe from as low as possible, not over the top of the position.

After the snipers advise the sniper control area of their location and field of view, they must organize their gear so that it is readily accessible. The only gear that should be out is that being used at the moment. This makes an emergency exit more efficient. Systems for resting, observing, recording, reporting, eating, bathroom calls, etc., should be established, and the snipers should alternate duties every 30 to 60 minutes so they will remain effective for longer periods of time. Each person has a different threshold for fatigue. When a sniper becomes fatigued, he should say so, not wait until his eyelids flutter or his vision blurs or is kaleidoscoping in and out. At that point, he will be looking but not seeing.

CHANGING FIRING POSITIONS

The sniper, moving from firing position to firing position, runs the risk of offering target indicators to the adversary in exchange for a more advantageous location. But there are ways to reduce the risk of being detected.

When walking, the sniper must walk distinctly and carefully, being conscious of every step he takes. He should walk in a crouch to maintain a low profile with shadows and bushes—most adversaries will be looking for an upright man. When crawling, he should make sure his weapon's muzzle isn't plowing up dirt or sticking up in the air. He should not allow his head or buttocks to rise too high, and he should make sure his feet aren't hitting bushes or flopping around in the air. He must remain conscious of the fact that crawling is noisy, especially on rough surfaces.

When moving during the day, the sniper should always assume that he is under enemy observation. He should stop, look, and listen frequently, using his optics to look through his concealment and making sure he blends into his background before observing. He should move slowly and deliberately, staying alert and patient.

Before moving at night, the snipers must allow at least 30 minutes for their eyes to adjust to the darkness. If lights are to be used, they must have red lenses. If white lights pass overhead, the snipers should avoid looking at them and silhouetting themselves by moving in front of them. To distinguish an object in the dark, snipers should either get low to the ground to skylight it or look approximately 5 to 10 degrees off to one side. If they stare at the object, it will fade in and out and give a perception of movement. Objects appear farther away at night than they actually are due to diminished definition, so the snipers should use their free hand to feel for obstacles and rely on their other senses of smell and hearing. They should assume that the adversary has night vision devices and always use the terrain to mask their movement.

REPORTING INTELLIGENCE

Once they are in their positions, the sniper teams are ready to report target site intelligence. A good report is accurate, clear, concise, complete, and timely. The procedure is for one sniper to observe and whisper information as it is gleaned to his partner for recording. Once all the information is recorded, it is transmitted to the sniper commander. This procedure is efficient and enhances the report's accuracy. If the sniper observes activity then tries to record it, he will miss information, or, if the sniper tries to observe and simultaneously transmit the information, the transmission will be too long and contain inaccuracies.

The information to be reported should include the time of the incident, the number of adversaries observed, physical descriptions of the adversaries, the activity, and the location. The SALUTE report (see Chapter 4) is a good system to use when recording and reporting information. Sniper teams may design suspect pattern analysis forms containing these elements of essential information so they can just fill in the blanks. Figure 15 is an example of such a form. The sniper commander plots the information in an attempt to identify an adversary's pattern.

THE PREDICTABLE TARGET
AREA AND TARGET ASSIGNMENT

In most adversary/hostage situations, a predictable target area will develop. As the term suggests, a predictable target

TIME (When Observed, Not When Transmitted):

NUMBER OF PERSONNEL OBSERVED:

PHYSICAL DESCRIPTION:

    Race

    Gender

    Age

    Height

    Weight

    Clothing

DISTINGUISHING CHARACTERISTICS:

EQUIPMENT/WEAPONS:

ACTIVITY:

LOCATION:

Figure 15: Suspect pattern analysis.

area is one in which the adversary is expected to appear. The development of a predictable target area will normally require the sniper teams to shift into new positions overlooking this area. For example, the sniper teams are set up in 360-degree coverage when a demand is made by the adversary for a car to be parked near the front door in two hours. A predictable target area has developed: in two hours, the adversary will leave by the front door and go as quickly as possible to the car. The sniper commander should coordinate the snipers' positions and duties with the predictable target area and the time of the vehicle delivery to enable the snipers to overwatch the delivery officer. The sniper commander will inform the sniper team leader of the predictable target area and transfer control to him. To alleviate confusion, the sniper team leader should announce on the radio three times, "I am in charge, I am in charge, I am in charge." He then instructs one of the teams to shift to the predictable target area so there is a 2:1 sniper-to-adversary ratio. The sniper team leader sets up in the predictable target area also to observe. Figure 16 illustrates the sniper teams' positions before the shift, and Figure 17 illustrates the sniper teams' positions after the shift.

It is doubtful the adversary will leave the stronghold by any route other than the most direct one to the vehicle. But if this should happen, the outer containment officers can prevent his escape, or, if necessary, the emergency entry team can take him out.

At this point, no one is to use the radio except the sniper team leader, Alpha team, and Delta team. The only exceptions are for life-saving traffic or cancellation of the open-air assault by the sniper commander, SWAT commander, or anyone in the department who is responsible for ordering the mission. The sniper team leader then assigns targets to the sniper teams. Each sniper in the team is assigned a target to enable overlapping fields of fire. For example, if Alpha 1 cannot get target #1, Delta 1 will. The same goes for Alpha 2 and Delta 2 with target #2 (See Figure 17).

THE SHOT

Head shots are not the only way to solve the problem. If the adversary's head is obstructed, the snipers may have to shoot for his chest, stomach, hip, arm, or leg, but these alternate targets may require follow-up shots. This does not mean that you shoot to wound. The idea is to open the impact area for additional shots as required. The rationale in this situation is that if the sniper shoots for the adversary's head but the shot is obstructed, the adversary may escape or SWAT team members may have to engage him in close-quarter battle. Neither is acceptable if the sniper can get a round on target. Rest assured that when a .308 168-grain boat-tail hollow-point bullet rips through the adversary's pelvic bone, he won't be thinking about his hostage. Snipers should be aware that their teammates may be entering their fields of fire, and

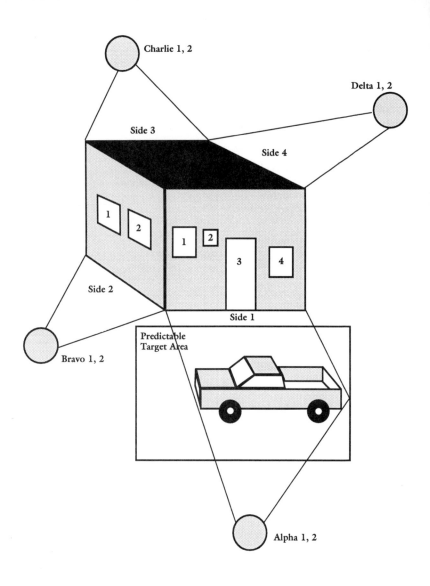

Figure 16: Predictable target area. In this example, the adversary has asked for a car to be delivered to the front door. This predicts the area where he will appear—he will leave by the front door and go as quickly as possible to the car. Before the shift, only one team is covering the predictable target area.

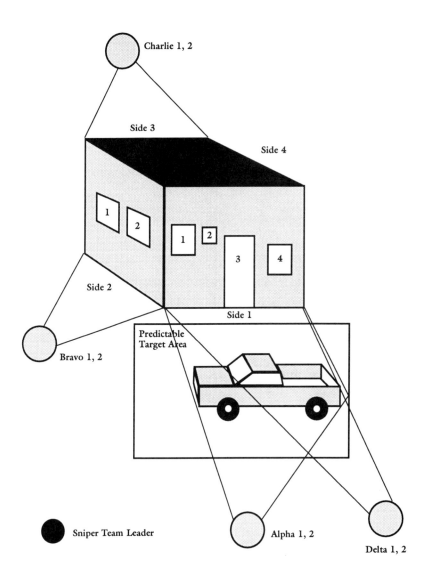

Figure 17: After sniper position shift. The sniper team leader is in position for the observation and fire commands, and he has chosen to leave Bravo and Charlie teams in place and shift Delta team to side one. This setup provides a 2-to-1 sniper-to-adversary ratio and overlapping fields of fire.

they should be careful when applying follow-up shots. A threat must still exist before any follow-up shots are undertaken, and only the minimal number of shots required to solve the threat should be fired. *Deciding whether to shoot is the shooter's responsibility.*

Many circumstances can cause snipers to decide not to shoot. They include an improperly identified target, an obstructed view, dead space, a hostage in the way, or noncompliance with the department's deadly force guidelines.

DEBRIEFING

Once the all clear is given, and after the snipers have accounted for and policed all gear, they may rally at the target site or rendezvous elsewhere for extraction. The sniper team leader debriefs the snipers, covering the mission from beginning to end, and then each sniper will debrief all concerned on their actions. Debriefing is essential for litigation, investigation, and a discussion of lessons learned. The snipers then service, maintain, and store their gear. They can then choose between going for a beer or going to bed—I bet on the bed!

CHAPTER SIX

TRAINING

To adequately cover sniper team training, I would have to write a separate book entirely on this subject. However, I'll hit the high points here.

ANALYZE DEPARTMENTAL NEEDS

First, the department's needs must be analyzed. Are most of the department's duties performed in urban or rural environments? If urban, the focus should be on overt entries into building hides. If rural, the focus should be on camouflage and stalking into hides. Most SWAT teams operate in environments with both urban and rural elements, which require a mix of training. If this is the case, the team leader or commander must decide which set of skills will be stressed in training. To do this, he must consider prior missions, looking at time-on-target, distances, situations requiring sniper assistance, and solutions.

PERSONNEL SELECTION

Personnel should be selected in a structured, consistent manner. Care must be taken in the selection process to ensure that only the highest quality personnel are chosen. As can well be imagined, having a marginal performer on a team will magnify liabilities. Another point of concern is the cost of training and equipping each sniper. Longevity in the position is desirable, but procedures should be established for replacing personnel due to substandard performance or attrition.

The Selection Process

Sniper candidates must:

Volunteer. Staffing of this position must not be forced, and personnel should not be chosen solely on their seniority.

Be a current SWAT member. Prior tactical training shortens training time and enables smooth transitions back into SWAT teams if the sniper option isn't used.

Be physically fit. Review the volunteer's scores on the department's regular tests to determine fitness.

Shoot 90 percent on a police rifle course. This indicates that the volunteer has a solid shooting foundation to build on.

Pass an oral review board. The review board should consist of the SWAT commander, sniper commander, and sniper team leader. The review board must decide how much value to place on each question. Some sample questions are as follows:

1) Why are you interested in sniper training?
2) What are your views on the department's deadly force policy?
3) Can you employ a surgical shot if required? (Board members may wish to have the volunteer flip through pictures of gunshot victims when asking this question.)
4) Do you smoke? (Smoking reduces night vision, compromises the sniper's position, and causes nervousness or inattention due to cravings.)
5) Do you consume alcoholic beverages? (Alcohol reduces night vision.)
6) How do you maintain your physical fitness?
7) Do you like the outdoors? (This applies mostly to rural environments. The sniper can't be distracted by darkness, dirt, animals, etc.)
8) Do you hunt? (A lot of stalking, camouflage, hide techniques, and tactical movements are learned this way.)

9) Do you enjoy shooting rifles? (The weapon of choice for many snipers is the rifle.)
10) How long do you intend to remain a sniper?
11) Do you have any military or police experience, photography skills, or other experience that should be considered?

Possess personal attributes such as:
Patience
Maturity
Loyalty
A can-do attitude
Reliability
Sound decision-making abilities

TRAINING

Sniper candidates must pass a qualification course in order to function as snipers. The course is based on the same standards as their training. If a sniper candidate fails to achieve these standards, he is not qualified. All training should be based on the one-shot-equals-one-stop concept, which stresses that the goal of each shot taken is immobilization of an adversary, and preparing for real situations should be stressed throughout the program. The training should be varied and challenging and should include the following skills:

1) Weapon and scope maintenance. These should be inspected frequently.
2) Data (dope) books. These should be inspected frequently.
3) Fundamentals of marksmanship
4) Short, mid-range, and long-range applications of rifles at determined and undetermined distances
5) Shooting positions, both supported and unsupported
    Prone—slung, unslung, and rollover
    Sitting—slung, unslung, Indian-style, and target-style
    Kneeling—slung, unslung, high, low, and schoolboy
    Squatting—slung and unslung

Hawkin

Standing—slung, unslung

Differences in terrain, hide construction, and situations where the sniper can get caught while moving require proficiency in a variety of shooting positions, which should be mixed into the qualification course.

6) Stress shooting. This induces mental and physical tension during training. A good way to induce mental and physical stress is to begin the qualification course with a stress shot. For example, the sniper must start 150 yards out, run forward 50 yards to the 200-yard line, load one round, and shoot a threat target in a credit-card-sized kill zone located 100 yards away within 25 seconds. To heighten stress, place a numerical value on the test so that if the sniper misses he automatically fails to qualify.

7) Tracking, ambushing, or tracking and holding methods on moving, reactive, turning, and pop-up targets

8) Elevated and angle shots

9) Night-firing techniques

10) Shoot/No-shoot targets

11) Internal, external, and terminal ballistics

12) Range estimation techniques

13) Observation techniques

14) Target site reporting procedures

15) Tactical planning

16) Camouflage techniques

17) Stalking and individual movement

18) Selection and occupation of firing positions

19) Hide construction and equipment

20) Coordinated target selection and firing techniques

21) Kim's (keep in mind) game—this hones the four elements of observation:

Awareness

Understanding

Recording

Response

22) Maintenance of all assigned equipment

Frequency of Training

Continual training is the only way to ensure mission success. Small amounts of regular training are more beneficial than infrequent sessions requiring many rounds. If possible, the sniper should be issued his weapon so he has access to it and can train whenever time allows. This training should be in addition to, not in lieu of, organized formal training. I recommend group training once a month, which includes a cold bore shot and group shots at various ranges. Formal, documented, semi-annual requalifications should be performed.

THE VALUE OF SNIPER TEAMS

As a sniper commander or team leader, if you want to sell your administration on the value versus the cost of maintaining a sniper team, explain the proper utilization of a sniper team and demonstrate it in SWAT exercises. Keep in mind that making shots is not the only value of having snipers. Attach them to all SWAT exercises as scouts, and get team leaders and others in the hierarchy thinking about their use. Then, once these officers use the snipers, they will be hooked. Once the team leaders understand the intelligence-gathering capabilities of the sniper teams, you can demonstrate their various sniper solutions and assists. First, complete a subject neutralization and then a multiple-subject neutralization. Next, perform a sniper-initiated vehicle assault, a sniper-initiated building assault, an overwatch operation, and a hostage snatch. You can train for situations as complicated as your coordinating abilities allow. Practice, practice, practice, and always try to achieve more.

INDEX

L

Line of departure (LOD), 21, 23-25, 41, 47, 67

M

Magnum eyebrow, 34
Mission, 21-22, 35, 37, 39-41, 45, 47, 55, 58, 63
Movement, 8, 34, 37, 48-49, 53, 62

N

Night vision, 3-4, 43, 53, 60
Noise, 4, 47
Numerical system, 10, 11

O

Obstacles, 8, 35-36, 50, 53
Operations order, 40-41
Open-air assault, 19, 30, 55
Outlines, 48
Overwatch, 38, 54, 63

P

Penlight, 4
Phase lines, 21-25, 42, 45, 49-50
Planning, 7, 31, 37, 39, 41-43, 45, 49-50, 62
Poncho, 3
Predictable target area, 15, 19, 30, 51, 53-57
Primary weapon, 2

R

Radio, 5, 16, 19, 21-22, 26, 30, 42, 45-46, 54-55
Range card, 20

Range finder, 5
Reflection, 48
Reporting intelligence, 53
Rifle maintenance, 3
Rifle scope, 2
Rules of engagement (ROE), 41, 44

S

T

SWAT
SNIPER

Deployment and Control

Tony L. Jones

Paladin Press • Boulder, Colorado

SWAT Sniper: Deployment and Control
by Tony L. Jones

Copyright © 1995 Tony L. Jones

ISBN 0-87364-856-0
Printed in the United States of America

Published by Paladin Press, a division of
Paladin Enterprises, Inc., P.O. Box 1307,
Boulder, Colorado 80306, USA.
(303) 443-7250

Direct inquiries and/or orders to the above address.

Cover photo: source unknown.

SWAT
SNIPER